Cadence

Giselle Robinson

For the Poets…
For the welcome.
In your world I have found the perfect fit.
No explanations required.
Thank you.

Acknowledgments

Thanks to Anthony Emanuel, for finding me after decades, reading my words, and having far more confidence in my work and ambition for my future than I ever had for myself. For the website he created out of that ambition over many 2AM phone calls.

To the poet Natasha Carrizosa. For my first feature and her relentless insistence that my place on the mic had always been there, just waiting for me.

To the poet AJ Houston. For sharing his wealth of knowledge and putting up with my litany of questions and my artist's need for constant reassurance with unending patience.

To my sister, Lorelli Mitchell. For all of the beautiful photos of our home, St. Thomas, USVI.

To my knowledge, this is the first poem ever written for me and the most moving gift I've ever received.
Written by a wonderful poet and loving friend, Christopher "Chris Key" Woodson, while he listened to my tears...

∾ Rainy Night ∾

Tonight, amidst a flood of tears, a storm of ailment
Her accent loses its spice
Uses energy reserved for heartbeats - to weep
Unwanted rain - but from the heavens, nevertheless

Tonight, she is not the searing glow of liquid razor blades
She is fuseless dynamite, oarless boat, riderless horse
Does not know that she does not need them
Unwanted rain – but from the heavens, nevertheless

Tonight, spring air finds her pale and pure
Only grief to clothe her naked soul
Helpless slave to the warmth it doesn't provide
Unwanted rain – but, nevertheless, from the cleansing heavens above

Introduction

I must tell you how we met. It was a night in September. At a spot downtown called Embargo. That night I read the poem – note to self. The only words from the poem that come to me now – this poem is a sign God uses regular moms - even if she is afraid to believe. Fast forward the memory. The music is coming through the speakers. Poets are clamoring about. They share their lines and love. The audience is a sea. I am standing near a table by the window and here comes this natural beauty. This quiet hurricane of a woman – Giselle.

I know this before she speaks. Before I read her lines. Before I learn her movement. She is the dancer from Gibran's book – The Wanderer.

༄

Once there came to the court of the Prince of Birkasha a dancer with her musicians. And she was admitted to the court, and she danced before the prince to the music the lute and the flute and the zither. She danced the dance of flames, and the dance of swords and spears; she danced the dance of stars and the dance of space. And then she danced the dance of flowers in the wind. After this she stood before the throne of the prince and bowed her body before him. And the prince bade her to come nearer, and he said unto her, "Beautiful woman, daughter of grace and delight, whence comes your art? And how is it that you command all the elements in your rhythms and your rhymes?"

༄

Rhyme is what brought us together. Roots are what keep us together. We share some of the same loves. The page. The stage. Tragedy and Triumph. The salt in the sea. The sand in the men we have landed and loved. Our family trees that have shaded and sheltered us. We are each other. I think. She is a blessing. I know.

I have this bright idea to start an open mic – natty roots and rhyme. Gi is laying on my living room floor and I am giving her all of the crazy in my head. She is giving it right back. I am ranting about the mess I have gotten myself into with starting this natty roots thing. I need a savior and Gi is it. She will be the first feature poet of natty roots & rhyme. She gave me all of the reasons she wasn't right for the part. And in her words – I juss come! (I just came. She used to throw that phrase around like a get out of jail free card. It never got her out of reading a poem or getting on stage. She just thought it would.) She gave me a real good tongue-lashing and still curses me today. But, she did it. And she has not stopped. Something deep inside tells me she never will.

In the poem What If Giselle writes: What if our greatest gift from God was words and we never wrote them down?

God. What if she never wrote them down? There would be no Burns. Hard Truth. Clarity. There would be no Unrelenting Poetry. Poet on the Mic. Poet Love.

If she never wrote them down, you would never taste the salt in the Caribbean Sea. Know the love in the heart of the poet Gi. You would never read these lines from her life, her poem –

∾ Phantom Dance ∾

The burn, the flight
The landing so light
That ignite the fire within
To soar above the pulsing beat
To make art on aching bleeding feet
To hold, to move in unnatural ways
To reach and fold and bend and sway

And you would never know what the dancer told the prince.

∾

"Mighty and gracious Majesty, I know not the answer to your questionings. Only this I know: The philosopher's soul dwells in his head, the poet's soul is in the heart; the singer's soul lingers about his throat, but the soul of the dancer abides in all her body."

∾

Giselle Robinson is a philosopher. A poet. A singer. A dancer. Her words make us bend and sway. She is gracious and majestic. She is the truth. Truth is, God uses regular moms even if she is afraid to believe.

Believe me. There is only one Giselle. And the only poet that writes/makes me feel this way.

One love,
natasha carrizosa (natty)

Contents

∽ Slam ∽

∾ **Poet's Fuel** ∾
(A Bit of Suffering is Mandatory)

one

Rhythms of Home

Time and distance
Make cloudy the space
Between memory
And imagination
Truth hides in the fog

Cadence

I speak in the voice
Of my island home
Evoking the heat of the tropical sun
And the trade winds that blow
That flow
Thru my soul
Even when I am far from home

I speak in the cadence
Of my native land
In the rhythm of calypso
Rolling off of steel pan

I speak in tones of passion
To reflect my West Indian soul
Rising, dipping, rolling
Like the paths in the hills
Where I used to roam

I speak in terms
As colorful as the rainbow
For I see in color
Not judge by color

I see those hills, impossibly green
Trees rooted in the richest brown soil
Or in hard packed dry clay
Or standing straight up on the black rocky cliffs
That stand watch over our sea

The breathless wonder of the Caribbean Sea
Itself a blend of color few are blessed to see
Cool inviting blues or greens…or blues
Ever shifting ever changing

Cadence

Smooth like Baron
Poundin' hard as Machel
Never predictable
But predictably West Indian

And I see in red
That is the color of my family
In blood, my blood
That makes me part of them
And them of me
Forever pumping to the tune
Of a Sparrow melody
Not in white or black or brown or yellow
That's an American thing baby

Through the years we've been taught
As kids at home like to say...to yank
As in speak like a Yankee
Wash the color
The cadence
From your voice
So you can sound like them
Be like them
Be accepted by them
That is one lesson I refused to learn

For I speak as the trade winds flow
I speak in the cadence of Caiso
I speak with the passion of Cruzan rum
I speak in the color of the Caribbean sun

Born in Eden

Born in Eden
God's hand
In your face
Screaming red hibiscus
Flaming flamboyant
Draw hummingbirds
God's hand
Iridescent
In your face

Immersed in Eden
Traversing hills
On donkey back
Anansi tales
Teach crick crack
Children sing
In bare feet beat
Brown skin girl
Stay home and mind baby

Waking in Eden
Sweet sugar apples
Are green not red
And brown sugar you learn
Melts in the rain
Gyul cover yo head
Before you mess up yo straight

Sunsets in Eden
After majestic sun falls

Cadence

Pitch black nights
To highlight the stars
God's hand
Always and again
In your face

But in Eden's dark night
Soucouyant and Jumbies
Are never far
Holy water kept
Close at hand

Grown now in the Eden of my birth
Done learned the hardest lesson of all
Serpents don't slither
They walk straight and tall.

Island Time

There is water
In the air here
It rests on skin
Like a cloak
Renders escape
From heat
Impossible.
Flower scented
Tropical breeze
Made cooler
Sweeter
By dampened skin
Disguises the weight
Of wet heat.
It's absence magnifies
The thickness
Of sea soaked air
Laying there
On your skin
A damp cloak
Slowing motion
Amending urgency
Setting Island Time.
'Til the breeze returns
Allowing moments
Of carefree movement
Unencumbered
By the heat
And weight
Of water filled air.

Simplicity

Simple pleasures
Sand squiggled between toes
Salty sea soaked fingers on your tongue
Naked and free under tropical sun
Cool droplets of the Caribbean
Dribbled from mommy's hand
Over a sun warmed back

Big sister captures an ocean
In her palms
Making rain and rainbows
Of her own
Water falls thru upheld hands
A child's unspoken praise
And prayer to her Maker
For the blessing of being
Born in Paradise

Black Don't Crack

Shoulders squared
She stands
Straight and strong
Strength of generations
Generations of hardship

Bent low to pick
The whitest cotton
Wielding her machete
Thru fields of cane
To make the whitest sugar
Bearing babies on her back
Beautiful black babies

'Til the blistering tropical sun
Falls slowly into the sea
A silent explosion of color
And the one who calls himself
"Master"
Turns his back
Satisfied with today's harvest
Of whitest cotton, whitest cane

She straightens from her labors
Black shoulders squared
Black chin held high
Ancient wisdom shines
In black eyes fixed on the horizon
Whispering truth
To the babe on her back

Cadence

Songs of praise on her lips
Singing halleluiah
To the one that set the sky ablaze
Hope held high
Halleluiah
Beauty is as beauty does

And the white man
Striding through his plantation
Will one day see
Black don't crack
Not to whip
Not to strap
Black don't crack

Baptized

In the tradition of thanks
She brings the child
Given to her by God
To the house of God
And offers him back

In the tradition of praise
The pastor lifts the wailing babe high
Give glory to the Most High
For new life
Only He can create

In the tradition of blessings
The babe is washed
In the waters of promise
Promise that the Creator will shower blessings
Even amid the fiercest storm

In the tradition of love
The family gathers
In one jubilant voice
Gives thanks and praise
To all Glory
For all blessings

Dry Season

So they stand
In the sea that surrounds
The life giving sea
Backs bent
Laboring to clean today's catch
In the very waters
From which it came
They talk of tonight's pot
"Who have provisions to boil with this fish?"
The dry season been long
The ground is so hard

Hard as life
And as unforgiving as
The life-giving, life-taking sea

Gon have to bake a dumb bread
To fill dem chirren belly
Dey always hungry
From runnin wile in de bush
Dey don't know
Dey don't know
Life is hard
Hard like de ground
In dry season.

Stolen Moments

Wey you goin gyul?
Ah goin go wash deze clothes
Awright den
Hurry up so you could come mind deze chirren
A nous allez. Vit vit
Okay Mommy
Grateful for the dirty bundle
She makes her escape… quickly
Before they can call her back
For yet one more urgent chore

Amidst the havoc of her family
The endless cacophony of voices
Old lady groaning the pains of age
Old man shouting his frustration
At the perpetual destruction
Wreaked by the latest generation
Of wildly screaming
Untamed children

She longs for silence
For peace, for calm
So that she can sink
Into the rustle of leaves as the trade winds blow
The soft thud of the mangos falling from the trees
And wait to see the guanas emerge from the bush
To feast gleefully
Before the old man can send kids
To steal the sweet fruit

Cadence

So grateful for the dirty bundle
She labors mindlessly in the small stream
Soap, scrub, rinse
Soap, scrub, rinse
Dreaming a girl's dream
Of endless love and faraway lands
Only in those moments of stolen peace
Can she hear her own words
Can she hear her own voice
Can she be a poet

My Best Friend's Wedding

The baby is sleeping next to me
Beads of sweat cover his head
Soaking little Afro curls
Laying them as flat and straight
As Arawak tresses
It's funny how he only sweats in his sleep.

The power is out again
But at this moment
No one on the hillside
Has cranked up their generator
To disturb the silence
In the name of convenience

Only echoes of wind chimes on distant porches
And the gentle flap of clothes on the line
Play the lullaby that keeps
Sweet baby asleep.

My niece is on the porch playing word games
She has volunteered to chase the cricket when he wakes up
There's a reason why God gives babies to young people.

My parents are making the most
Of this quiet hour
There is another wedding tonight
Rhea, my best friend of many years
Mommy's honorary daughter
Today is her day.

Cadence

There were bride tears this morning
Fears of a darkened church
No electricity to light her way
We dried her tears and I heard my sister say
We'll bring candles if need be
To light your way
Mark awaits at the end of the aisle
In truth, that is light enough.

My family and yours
Will dance at your wedding
Even if we have to sing our own tune.

two

For the Love of Words

Sticks and stones
Can break your bones
But words
Words can break your heart

~

I take my shelter under poets wings,
Find solace in the words they free unto winds,
Winds that surround, echoing poets' sound,
Caress and console my ancient infant soul,
Turning fears into tears
That I may bleed this lessons verse,
Send it back to the wind,
Its a poet's thing,
To give shelter and wings
To the universe....

Poet Love

I love like… Epic
Encompassing and endless
Love both hero and villain
Relentless
No pretty Sonnet or witty Haiku
Could portray both the hero and villain in you

I mourn in broken lines
No longer joined
By your 'love you', 'want you'
Pen unfinished stanzas
On shredded pages
Over holes left behind
That were once filled by you

I bleed in ink
Spill my hurt as hate
Eager audience awaits
Each haunted by hurts of their own
Spit my rage on mics
In bright stage lights
And thank God for slam

I come in verse
Writhing rhythm and rhyme
Draw your heat
To my beat
And then coda, repeat
That's what happens
When you fuck with a Poet.

Poet On The Mic

There is a spark in his eye
Warmed by a sweet sexy smile
Fanned to life by the passion of his word, his art
It begins to take root in my heart

I feel the slow burn begin
A silent shiver on my skin
A flush of warmth
From my lips to my thighs
Stoked by that spark in his eyes

For so long, it seems
I've been so cold
What might it be like
To feel him take hold
Of my small soft frame
Against all that heat
My mind reels
As my heart skips a beat

In the midst of the crowd
My breasts swell and strain
Hoping not to moan out loud
Forgotten passion drenches me
Like a warm tropical rain

Still standing at the mic
His talented tongue
Spits the passion of his art
My thighs yearn to part

Do I dare touch that flame
Dare to know that passion no woman could forget?
Would it be better to wake with the scars from that burn
Or to live in the icy numbness of regret?

Tossing his head
His eyes catch mine
And that spark sears my soul

I close my eyes
Afraid of the heat
But his voice still stokes passion
So hot
So sweet

Trapped now by that fire that burns from within
I feel his locks trail over my dampened skin
Following that path of fire
As hot lips trace the heat of my desire

Skim down my neck
Suckle at my aching breast
Lower
Lower, as my soft belly quivers
A trail of wet kisses
Relentless
In pursuit of my…
Damn

I hear the voice of Cassandra Wilson
As, oh yes – he Moves me
Moves over me
Under me
Deep so deep in me
Thighs tremble
Thighs tremble

Burned now by that flame
I cry out his name
And I moan out loud
In the midst of the crowd

What If...

I write because I have to
Words too often penned in blood
Ripped without mercy from my soul

I spit because I have to
To vent, to share, to hear from you
That my pain is not mine alone

I write and I spit
I listen to poets
Because words matter
Because words haunt
These questions haunt me...

What if
Our greatest gift from God
Was words
And we never wrote them down

What if
Our words only came in the form
Of questions...unanswered
So we never wrote them down

What if
Your questions could solve
Your brother's dilemma
But you never wrote them down

What if
Yesterday's words from God
Held tomorrow's blessings to a child
But we never wrote them down

What if
You learn your words are not from you
But never learn that they are not just for you
So you never wrote them down

What if
The answers you seek
A poet might speak
Any night on an open mic

What if
The pain of the man
You could never understand
Was poured out on an open mic

What if
A strong woman wailed
Her secret pain unveiled
Your plight on an open mic

What if
Youth spoke truths
You'd forgotten in time
Tonight on an open mic

What if
Poets spoke of love and pain
And truth cured shame
For honor not fame
To give to you
A balm of words
To soothe a wounded soul
What if the poets spoke
And no one listened

I pray that you be blessed today
By the words of a courageous poet
Who dared to pen their pain on pages
And bare their soul to you on an open mic

Unrelenting Poetry

I love to get lost
In a book…
In hundreds of pages
Thousands of words
And immerse myself
In the author's world

Five hundred words
Set the scene
As we slip into
The writer's dream

But when a poet
Takes the mic
For three short minutes in time
They can wound or heal
And make me feel
Exposed within their rhyme

In a word
A verse
A moment freeze
Lay bare my own
Insecurities

Despite my most
Impassioned plea
The poet speaks my soul
Allows no moment of ennui
My passions they unfold

The secrets I won't tell myself
Are shouted from the stage
No longer hidden on a shelf
Unmask my pain and rage

And in that moment I am free
My life on stage not just in me
Thank God they did not hear my plea
But spoke their heartfelt poetry

And allowed me in that moment just to be
Just to be
To be
Free

Phantom Dance

When familiar voices sing and play
Haunting melodies of long past days
When piano notes strike bone deep key
Muscles ache to move to remembered sway

Laying flat on the coolness of sheets
Tapping toes mark rhythm in air
Restless finger keep staccato beat
On ancient aching abs

In the stillness of the Texas night
A phantom dance begins
Muscles move to memory
Muscles move like memory

Toes pointed, heel up, belly and ass tucked tight
Arms raised, extend, extend
The screaming burn lives everywhere
Now chin up and smile

Smile, because this burn
This burn
Will let you defy gravity
Spin with blinding perfection
Dizzying to crowds, but not to you
It is the music in your muscles
That makes your head spin

The burn, the flight
The landing so light
That ignite the fire within
To soar above the pulsing beat
To make art on aching bleeding feet
To hold, to move in unnatural ways
To reach and fold and bend and sway

The ripple runs through ribs
Fire rages in rock hard thighs
Fluid arms flow
Defying bones that x-rays show

I feel the phantom dance
In muscle flesh and bone
Feel the power of the burn rush through
That few have ever known
Now it is the heart that bleeds
Not battered bloodied toes
In the stillness of the Texas night
Longing to fly to spin head high
To once again bone and gravity defy
To ride to sweet adrenaline high
To smile as the fire burns

But only the phantom dances tonight
Only memory haunts joint and bone
This body no longer answers the call
Gravity wins today
So bittersweet the memory
To feel the phantom
Swirl and sway.

For The Artist

~Written to Round Midnight by Theloneous Monk
As performed by Bobby McFerrin~

This is for the art
This is for the artist
The musician
The notes
The verse
That play for us
Life's melody, its rhythms, its harmony

This is for the art
For the artist
The poet
The words
The verse
That pen for us
Life's truths on pages

This is for the art
The artist
The actor
The character
The play
Life's lessons
Brought to life for us on stages

This is for the art
For the artist
The painter
The brush
The strokes
The scene
Framing dreams and memories

This is for Monk
For this song
For showing us Round Midnight
Covered 1000 times
Because artists honor
Passion, beauty, art

This is for Bobby McFerrin
For this song
For taking us Round Midnight
With his amazing instrument
Because artists honor
Passion, beauty, art

This is for the art
This is for the artist
This is for Jazz and for Scat
For Rhythm-n-Blues
For Reggae and Soca and Pan

This is for spoken word and poets on stages
This is for art we dared to bring to life
This is for the artists that broke ground
And lead the way

This if for Billie Holiday and Nina Simone
This is for Charlie Bird Parker, Duke Ellington
and Miles
This is for Bob Marley and the Mighty Sparrow
This is for Langston Hughes and Maya Angelou
This is for Mark Kelley Smith…So What
This is for Lena Horne and Sydney Poitier
This is for Basquiat

Cadence

This is for courage and dedication
This is for memories and dreams
This is for lessons and pain and joy and shame
This is for the artists who bring them to light and to life
This is for the artist
This is for the art

three

For Want Of Love

Haiku

Each time I gave love

It was handed back to me

On silver platters

∾

Haiku

He planted hope seeds

Watered them with make-believe

They are all dead now

The Sequel

See, when he drove off in the old car
I thought he'd bought it
Hell, I bet you thought so too

He took that tired old heap
And tuned her up
Real sweet
Aired up the tires
Changed her oil
And every time he turned that key
Her engine hummed... purred.

Made sense to me
That he'd chosen to buy
A Used Car
Because you see
He was not the most
Care-full driver

The absent-minded professor
Lost in a poem, a dream
A new acoustic riff
Would plow her into potholes
With unthinking abandon
Graze her hubs on curbs
Eyes on clouds
Not mirrors

The new rattles and clanks
Would inevitably draw his attention
Reminding him
That there's no such thing
As a free ride
That she'd break down
Without his care
And the cycle would begin
All over again

He abandoned her one day
On a lonely roadside
Said the cost of her care
Was not worth the ride
But as he took off
All swagger and stride
Back turned to the heap
He'd left behind
The new dents
That showed the imprint of
His care-less handling
Hoses leaking fluids
That ran only for him
His disregard so complete
He didn't realize
As he strode down that street
That the jingle in his pocket
Were her keys

Wide Awake

Lying here
Alone
In our bed
I dream you
Wide awake
Close my eyes
And ears
There is no world
To interfere
As I dream you
Wide awake
Clothes melt
Into memories
I feel the flesh of you
The heat of you
Wrapped around me
Nipples pucker
In this empty bed
As I feel your lips
Your teeth
You suckle
You nip
I moan
So wet
Feel your fingers
Strum
Pull oceans
From my depth
Feel your breath
On my neck
Feel you
Loving me

Taste your length
On my tongue
My throat opens for you
Feel you grow
My thighs are wet
I am so ready for you
I dream you
Wide awake
You fill me
I can feel it
So tight
So perfect
You fit me
Perfect
This empty room
Fills with the moans
You draw from me
You make me feel
Perfect
Can't breathe
All my senses
Filled with you
By you
Wrapped so right
Around me
Wrapped so tight
Inside me
I feel you
I dream you
Wide awake
I miss you
Like air

Terrifying

Sometimes
You protect yourself
From me
So convincingly
It is easy to believe
There is no there
There
That we love like friends
That we fuck like fiends
That there is no 'in' in your love

Sometimes
I ride you
Ferociously
Frantically
Trying to beat down
That wall you've built
With my hips
With my lips
I am wide open to you
You feel closed to me
It is terrifying
To feel alone out here
Naked
On top
Of that wall you've built

Cadence

Sometimes
The wall I feel
Feels like you
Loving me
And we are safe
Inside
I am safe
In your love
It is terrifying
Free falling
Through thin air
Trusting you'll be there
To catch me.

Wonderful

You are a wonderful woman
You have so much love to give
You were good to me
Good for me
It saddened me
That I could not love you back
I know one day
Some wonderful man
Will give you the love
You deserve
It just won't be me

Five times I have heard this
Well, technically four
Four and a half decades
I have drawn breath on this earth
Just as surely
I'll hear it once more

I have heard it in his silence
Seen it in his reticence
I love with every part of me
Only fools throw it away easily
It is hard to lose a good
Hooker/maid/chef /nurse/secretary
Especially when she works for free

But I hear it in his silence
Feel it in his reticence
Loving me back
Is a higher price
Than he's willing to pay

So soon
One day
He too will find the words to say
You are a wonderful woman
I know a good man will love you
One day

Bath Time

The candles are dying
They have given their all
Burned with full intensity
They were never made
To be replenished
Only to give light
Burn bright
Die silently
Darkness
A brief burst
Of pungent smoke
The only signs
Of their demise
They will not be missed
But in odd moments
They will be remembered fondly
Then replaced

The wine bottle too
Is almost empty
Designed only to give
A short reprieve
To breaking parts
Broken hearts
It's asking price paid
Up front
It's thanks filled with flowers some days
Most likely praised to porcelain gods
Rewarded in recycling bins

The tub is a different story
She has been replenished
Time and again
Since this night we met
She can hold no heat on her own
Bubble-less now
What would be the point
In restarting the popping
Of make believe joys
We already know
How this story ends
How make-believe pretties
Explode and die
When confronted with truth and air

The cigarettes at least
Are plentiful
Soothing in their moments
If deadly in the end

It's bath time
Rubber ducky has been passed down
To the innocents
This is where grown women come
To cry

Unadorned

He loves me
He loves me not
He loves me
He loves me not

One by one
Picture perfect petals
Plucked and discarded
On the cold unyielding ground

Ground
Cold, unyielding
Petals plucked
Still not revealing

He loves me
He loves me not

Till all that remains
Is stem and core
Not so pretty anymore
Unadorned
By picture perfect petals
Of hope

In Silence

Yesterday
The rain had no sound
The sun enticed
But held no warmth
To banish winter's chill

I stared longingly
Into the crisp bright sky
And called the sun a lie

Last night
I found warmth
In moonlit lips
In silence
Heard echoes
Of raindrops on tin

Not My Style

I don't write love poems
Pretty sure I don't know how
I have known love
I'm sure I did
But that was years and miles
From now

Back in the day
When love lived in him for me
And in me for he
When the sun that lit the sky
Was born in my heart
And the leaves in the trees
Were stirred by his whispered pledge
Love forever

My mind
My moments
My muse
Were dedicated
Devoted
To anticipation
Exceeded only
By reality

Sweet secret smiles
Just for me
Just for he
Entrenched in rapture
In bliss
All hope and promise
Encased in a kiss
So I had no need to write

Cadence

Then he was gone
Love was gone
Well, his anyway

And my fingers flew over keys
Pounded out my pain on pages
Blood gushed forth from my pen
Soul naked
Bared for all to see
But still
I did not write of love

Ten thousand words
My life in print
A seemingly endless saga
Of agony, abuse, isolation, torment
All the way to crazy and back again
Well… maybe not quite all the way
Back again

But to pen the current of my story
To see the truth of it on paper
Would drown my deluded dreams
And I would surely not survive
So I could not write

Many years have passed
Since love left me broken
And the hole in my heart
Has long since mended
But he did not break it cleanly
So the scars still ache sometimes

It is a curious ache to me now
Here in his wake
For where passion once warmed
And pain once burned
Lies a bit of a chill

Men walk by
And don't look anymore
Love lives years and miles
From here

So I don't write love poems
I'm pretty sure I don't know how

Haiku For Him

He calls me intense.
It is true. I am. This is my
Journey into him.

He says my "crazy"
Is what makes me a poet.
It is true. I am.

I will speak my heart
With hands, feet, back, arms and legs.
I pray you see love.

Silvered glass reflects
Wrinkled flawed imperfection
His eyes reflect grace.

In My Eyes

You grasped the darkness from your soul
To cast this shadow over me
As like knows like
Your soul recognized my scars
You saw you in my eyes
The you that you despise

The endless victim of those
Who should have cherished
Who beat you down
Till light and hope perished

Knew that I would take your lash
Would not fight, nor moan nor thrash
Because I am you
The you that you despise

And all the pain you felt inside
That left you with no place to hide
Your unbearable agony, daily torment
Needed a soft target on which to vent

And in an answer to your prayer
God or Satan placed me there
Your soul recognized my scars
And you saw you in my eyes
Because I am you
The you that you despise

Burns

Ice crystals
Trapped in palms
Burns

Tropical sun
On pale smooth flesh
Burns

Hurricane winds
Whipped through trees
Burns

Ballet
Danced on carpet
Burns

Hurtful words
From mother's lips
Burns

You
Are flame

Your voice
Seductive passion
Melts phone lines
Sets imagination ablaze

Your eyes
Singe flesh
Unrestrained desire
Melts my core

Jolts
To my heart
Old dreams
Melt
To the heat
Of your flame

My soul
Alight
Is light
This light
Your light
Your flame
Burns me alive

Hard Truth

Why can't I write
A serious poem
About feeling
Un-desired
Un-desirable?

On the night I was stood up
For the 3rd time
By the same man
I wrote "Used Car For Sale"
You know… 'can't give this shit away'
And I smiled when the crowd laughed
At my shame

Why can't I write
A serious poem
About feeling
Un-wanted
Un-want-able?

Laying out in the sun
In my teeny bikini
Gearing up to get on that night's mic
I wrote "Shit Out Of Luck"
Because I knew that I'd come home alone
Again and always…alone
And I smiled when the crowd laughed
At my pain

Why can't I write
A serious poem
About feeling
Un-loved
Un-love-able?

When it ends
When they leave
After the blink of an eye
A minuscule moment of time
I pen my pain, my angst, my shame
I write about "My Muse"
I write it's "Not My Style"
And I know as I watch ink dry
I know in my heart, the why

I know in my heart the why
So…. why can't I write
A serious poem
About being
Un-love-able?

Because some truths are too hard
To be seen on pages
To be spit on mics
Some truths are too hard
Some truths are too hard.

Clouds Of Dust

Lessons learned
Now engrained
Buried deep
In bone and brain
Dust cloud of past pain

Old scars
Draw new wounds
Memory calls
From bone deep tomb
Coloring sight and sound

Empty arms
Welcome heat
Stone ground hearts
Recoil, retreat
Dust clouds rise
Dark waves of warning

Replay, repeat
Pain-filled learning

Shades and windows
Locked tight
Don't forget to leave on a light
Purse, keys, smokes, cell
Last breath check
Ready set

Anticipation blends
With nerves, with fear
What will I say?
Was this right to wear?
Spine set stiff and straight in chair

Rejecting menacing memory
Reclaiming love's opportunity

Modern clock
Marks time in silence
No hands sweep its round face
Heartbeat metronome
Ticks loud in silence
LED lights proclaim disgrace

Starch stiffened spine
Softens, sags
Melts in a flow
Of hot slow tears
Twin paths score
Painted cheeks
Tandem highways
Disgust & Despair

Oh I am not lost
I know my way here
And the soundtrack plays familiar refrain
Pride and hope grind to dust
And settle dense clouds
In bone and brain

Press pause
Stop video stream
If I must live
If I must breathe
Then I must be brave
And dare to dream
Dare to dream
Dream warmth
Dream care

Cadence

Rational minds reason
New face, new soul, new day
Passion wakes from dormant season
Yearning soul does not know ration
Dust filled heart does not know reason

Battle for supremacy
Promised warmth
And pain filled legacy
Rings loud before the silent phone

His arrival does not banish
The tears of self-doubt
Born of dust clouds
In bone and brain

Razor edged whips
Lashed round body and soul
Trap tears
Preserving dignity

I say,
"I did not think you'd come"
He says,
"I thought you'd tear me a new one"
Told him, that's not how I roll

In warm embrace, though tears still burned
We agreed on lessons to be learned
What's her name does not live here
And what's his name is not sitting in that chair

A Perilous Sea

He comes to me
I am awash in jazz and poetry
Awakening to the sound of acoustic guitar
Drenches me in literature and history
My mind is nourished
Fills my pores
With his salty essence
My body he tosses about
In the joyful sway of his passion

I fear the perils of his sea
Have been battered by storms before
Have fought the power of waves
Have tried to capture that power
Even as I watched water seep
Thru clenched fist

I fear the perils of his sea
Even as wonder washes over me
For I know his ebb and his flow
And as I feel him come
I know he will soon go
For this is the way
Of his turbulent sea

Cadence

I fear the burn of his salty flow
Should I fall
Should his power bring me to my knees
Fear the rough sand
Of the seabed at my feet
That will abrade
Leaving tender flesh raw
Wounded, weakened, weeping
Greedily drawing more salt
My salt
Into its capricious depths

So I stand
Limbs loosely held
To bend and bow
And sway to his flow
Yet resist the dangers of the undertow
I heed the wise old siren's warning

I anticipate
Appreciate
The power
The wash
Of his waves return
And I choose to ride
This wave
His wave
I bend and bow
To his ebb and flow.

Foolish

He tempted me to hope
'Til I toyed with thoughts of being
Worthy of the warmth in his eyes
Eyes that shone with admiration
Appreciation

Then he slashed and sliced
With words of ice
(I am a poet. Words matter)
Till hope shriveled back
To its usual size
Pebbled in the pit of my belly
Useless and cruel by its very design
Poisonous and painful by its nature

I have shed no tears
What would be the point?
I have never been
Enough

༄

I have never been a cutter
You will find no razor scars on me
I slice at me
Internally
With the icy shards
Of my reality
He has given me new tools.

Thursday's Poem

The first time my shirt hit the floor
We had sex, good sex
Definitely worth repeating
Practicing, perfecting
Um, practicing…yeah

Since then, sometimes
We just straight up fuck
Grasp and grab
Bite and bang
Till my cervix is bruised in bliss

But the last time
Oh God…the last time
We…and we
And time passed
Unnoticed
Homage was paid
In touch
Soft and rough
And muffled screams
There was no line, no seam
No him, no me

A thousand tongues fluttered, traced
Music and moans melded to pulsing embrace
We had, it was, we made…

Can you help a poet out here?
Because we did not make love
Cannot make love
Where there is
No love
And we cannot feel love
According to his complex algebraic formula
Requiring that time equals X
And the rotation of the earth's axis reaches Y

Why oh why Lord
Did you send him to me?
The first one ever not to run from my crazy
The only one to look at my bony body
Muss up my wayward curls
And Then call me exotic beauty

Why Lord did you send me this
Relationship phobic artist
Who consults the almanac
To determine what he feels?

So we did not make love
Will not feel love
Because I sure as hell
Will not fall first
Been there done that
It is the worst kind of curse
To love first
To love most
To take the fall alone

But Lord,
I cannot recall ever feeling so
Accepted, broken and baggage and all
Being so cherished
Nurtured and nourished
Treasured and pleasured
And… Oh God.

But we did not make love
Surely we surpassed simple sex
Found far more than a frantic fuck
So the poet has no words

We
Tasted clouds
Touched dreams
Enchanted fairies
Rode moon beams
We made care
Melted time and wax
Danced on dampened sheets
Aware only
Of heartbeats

But we did not
Could not
Make love
So what would you call it
Can you help a poet out here?

The Ride

The right blend
Of curve and angle
Weight and pitch
Her natural tendency to fly
His predilection to flee
Set the coaster on its course

As onlookers cheered or gasped
Over near perfect
Always perilous
Contortions
Riders both nervous
Nearly nauseous
But both smitten by the glory
Of sun on skin
Wind in faces
Temporarily tossed caution
To that wind

Some subtle shift
In weight and wind and speed
Alerted them
Well at least
Alerted him
Of the perils entailed
In fearless flight

Cadence

Out of instinct
As natural as air
He set foot
To screeching, screaming
Brakes

Had she not still been lost
In the wonder of the ride
She might have been braced
For the sudden change of pace

Bruised now
Both ribs and knees
Still swirling head
And heart
Yet to yield to the reality
Of his new course and speed
She struggles to breathe
This heavier air
To find clarity of mind
To now decide
Should she deposit her coin
And continue to ride…

Nightlight

I love to watch him sleeping
Cocooned in my comforter
Even through the Texas summer
Shrouded from head to foot
No room under there for anything
But me

I talk in my sleep
He smiles in his
Those peaceful slumberous smiles
Assure me as no words ever could
Of his joy and comfort
In my bed

In his grief he sleeps restlessly
I see his fingers rest on lips
As though he tries to make sense
Of loss and pain
Even in dreams

Sunlight often reminds him
To mind his step
Keep his distance
But in sleep and in dreams
He reaches for me and pulls me close
I love to watch him sleeping

The Alchemist

He calls her
Alchemist
A lover's jest
A line from a rhyme
Naming her Power
Naming him Fear.

Fear
That she will conjure
While he sleeps
Weave her goddess
Touch in his mortal
Dreams and he will
Awaken bound by her
Threads of gold.

She smiles softly
Ancient woman's wisdom
Whispered down
Through the ages
From woman's heart
To woman's heart.

It is he who is
The wizard
His alchemist's skill
Refined from time
Before time

He who has taken
Common steel
Bathed it in
Acceptance
Showered it in
Reverence
Tooled it with
Patience
Until it emerged
From his embrace
Gleaming
Warm and rich and
Golden.

~ *four* ~
Slam

Haiku

Your silence screams loud

Clanging cymbals in my head

Words are balm to me

~

Haiku

I am thru begging

Enticing, pleading for touch

I am no Used Car

Preach

There is a new law governing our country these days
And Just in case you didn't get the memo
Let me fill you in:
If you say anything, ANYTHING
Loudly enough and often enough
It will – in fact – become – the Truth

Here is how it works
The President is a Muslim from Kenya
Obama's gonna kill your Grandma
Poor folks killed Wall Street
And on and on

And you know how it becomes the truth?
Because you don't care
Want to know how I know you don't care?
Because the Lunatics are louder than you!

Word plus Sound equals Power
If you know the real truth
Care about the real truth
Then Preach

When you hear the lies
Open the two good lips God gave you
And preach

Don't whine about the lunatics running the asylum
You put them there
Their torrent of lies
Drown out your pitiful cries
And your silence dooms us all

Preach
Because you know Kenyan is code for black
Preach
Because you know corporations are Not people
Preach
Because your Mama didn't raise no fool
To sit in the back of the bus
And give away all the rights
All the rights that Martin and Malcolm and Medger earned for us
thru sacrifice

My one year old nephew says "No"
Says it loud and clear
Because he's heard it so many times in his short life
Are we not as responsible
For our rights, our freedoms, our country
As we are for keeping the baby from playing in the damn toilet?

They want to kill the unions to silence our voice
Say it with me now
Hell No
They want people of color to produce
Super-duper ID's to prove our right to vote
Say it with me now
Hell No

If the loud-ass lunatics are the only voices we get to hear
Let me tell you your future:
You can't go to the doctor for birth control
Can't get an abortion
Can't get a bottle of milk to feed the baby they made you have
They will sit 80 kids in one class to learn the "facts" as determined
by the lunatic fringe
And when they are grown the will put ½ of them
In jails run by for profit corporations that need to keep your child
locked up for their quarterly earning statements
And oh yes
They will kill Grandma
Because the choice between food and medicine is death

This will be the price of your silence
Let this be the end of your silence
Meet loud lies with louder Truths
Preach with your voice
Preach with your vote
Preach my people
Preach

Used Car For Sale

(In the spirit of Calypso)

So listen
Here's the deal
I've got this car
And well
I've kinda had it forever
And when I was a little girl
It was actually just a little kids car
Just a toy…you know?
But for some reason
The big guys always wanted to play with my toy car
And well, since it wasn't big enough yet
They kinda fucked it up

So, here I am growing up with this fucked up car
And boy could it be a pain in the ass
Cuz even though she was broke
I couldn't get rid of the shit

Anyway, we developed what you could call
A love/hate relationship
Cuz you know
Now that I was grown
It was kinda cool when the big guys
Wanted to come over and mess with my car

Even if the shit was broke
They didn't seem to mind
They said my car was some
Sweet shit, baby

And that was alright
Cuz some of those brothers
Were fine as hell
And my car loved their asses
Under the hood
Revvin' the engine
And taking them curves hard baby

So a few years back
I got too sick to even think about the car
Then my son was so sick
The damn car just sat there
Parked up and neglected
But what's a girl to do?

Anyway
Damn car keeps on grumblin'
And tootin' at me
Reminding me that it needs some attention

But what the fuck?
I'm a girly girl
I ain't no mechanic

So anyway
I figure out how to get under the hood
Find some toys that looked like what them guys used
And got to work
I swear I tried
Mimicked all the moves I'd seen them guys do
And the fuckin' thing still won't turn over
But then,
I never could drive worth a damn

So I hit the streets to see
If any of these Texas men
Knew what to do under the hood
I mean
I know she's getting older
A little banged up
And rusty around the edges
So I threw in some incentive
Like – I can cook a mean pot
In trade for a little tune-up
Maybe a test drive?

After all these years
I cannot even believe
I can't give this shit away
So now I'm sittin' here
Listenin' to the shit moan about neglect
And I can't even work up the energy
To put them damned tools back under the hood

So what do you think girlfriend?
Is it time to call in the pros?
Ah fuck it
I'm just gonna put a sign in the rear window
Used Car For Sale

L'union Fait La Force

(For Haiti)

I searched and prayed for words
To honor what is happening in our world today
Found these words
In Creole
In the voice of Haiti
On the face of the Haitian flag

L'Union fait la force
In Union there is strength

L'Union fait la force
In Haitian hearts
L'Union fait la force
In the hearts of all peoples of the world
L'Union fait la force
For the people of Haiti

I spoke to my Mommy today
My heart bleeds for the motherless in Haiti
Saw Haitian men holding their heads
Unable to even bury their dead
Kissed my niece's baby
I cried for Haitian babies
L'Union fait la force

Through my tears
Images shown
Iceland, Taiwan
America, China, France
Amassed on Haitian soil
L'Union fait la force

In our world
Haiti defines poverty
Lives so harsh
We close our eyes
Too hard to see
L'Union fait la force

And the last shall be first
And the last shall be first
In the eyes of our God
In the hearts of our world
L'Union fait la force

Earth shook in Haiti
Skies were filled
With cries of pain
Tears flooded earth like rain
L'Union fait la force

There but for the Grace of God
Go I
Invades our hearts
As one people we cry
L'Union fait la force

Haitian people are survivors
Enduring brutal conditions each day
But on this day
On an island surrounded by water
Our brothers and sisters are dying…for water
Today they need more than our prayers
Even while we pray
Mon Dieu, laisser là guérit en Ayiti
Mon Dieu, laisser là guérit en Ayiti
My God, let there be healing in Haiti
L'Union fait la force

Clarity - September 21, 2011

Somewhere between
Heaven and Hell
I found
Understanding
Learned that
Bright glare and
Pitch dark night
Both impede
Clear sight

When I heard the news this evening
I felt a rush of joy
A sigh of satisfaction
He was dead
Justice was done

That blight on humanity
The one that had
So proudly
So cruelly
Dragged an innocent soul
Tearing, shredding him
Limb from limb
Would no longer draw breath
It was good
It was right

When I heard the news tonight
I felt my heart
Plunge
My stomach churned
He was dead
Could only find joy in knowing
His mother had not lived to see the day
Her innocent son
Was slain by the State
There was no justice
So much was wrong in my world

And there between
Heaven and Hell
There lived Epiphany
That moment of clarity
Of understanding
That the satisfaction found
In avenging James Byrd
Came at the price
Of Troy Davis's life

We flawed and imperfect beings
Can only create
A flawed and imperfect system
So let us leave
Justice and vengeance
To God

Disaffected Voter

Roses are red
Violets are blue
This poem is not for me
And I hope it's not for you

This poem is for the super cool
The super smooth
The geniuses that got the game all figured out
They are
Too smart, Too busy, Too tired, Too disgusted
TO VOTE!

Because Politicians suck
They all play the same game
Just a bunch of lying sharks
The good ole boys…
And… that don't have nothing to do with me
So why should I vote??

Let me tell you a secret
The Good Ole Boys love you so much
They have a special name for you
They call you the Disaffected Voter
So sick of the game - So slick to the game
You won't vote

Truth
There is no such thing as a disaffected voter
Not as long as you are breathing in America
From the light switch you turned on
To the A/C you can't afford
To the potholes in the road
That you can't buy gas to drive on
From your little brother that dropped out of the school
Because no one was paying attention
And you sister's fourth trip to the ER
Still hoping for medicine will soothe the baby
It is all affected

You know anyone who died in battle?
Got anyone behind bars being herded like cattle?
Are you sleeping in Mama's house
Because you can't find a job?
Are you hiding your car from the repo man
And screening for collection calls as best you can?
Tell me again how you are - Unaffected?

Yes the good ole boys rig it
And if you don't vote
They win
Can you dig it?
If you think your vote is
Use – less, Hope – less
They win

If you chose to…
Ball with your boys
Do your hair or your nails
Got nobody to watch the babies
Can't miss your show
Got clothes to wash on election day
They win

If you have never voted
Don't plan to vote
Please take your fist out of the air
Get Malcolm's name off your tongue
You give up the right to have it there
MLK is more than a holiday and a street in the hood
The Dream will die on the vine
If you don't vote for your own good

They are not all the same
Sure they all play the game
If you've got no elbows on the court
You lose
A guppy in a shark tank
Is called Lunch!
So Vote for the shark that's got your back

Ignorance is Not bliss
Ignorance is the Serpent's kiss
Enticing you to sit in your chair
And rail powerlessly that life is not fair

There is one day that you have
As much power
As the rich-est, slick-est, bad-est
The smartest good ole boy

Cadence

One way
That they are scared to death of you
Scared to death
That you will see the Dream thru

That you will Vote
For your child's education
Your right to see a doctor
Your right to own a home
Not a banker's right to own your soul
Your right to a job
Not a jail cell
They are scared to death that you will Vote

Roses are red
Violets are blue
This poem is not for me
And I hope it's not for you

In The Land Of Kings

I cringe when women write poems to kings
More so when men crown themselves
See I've known a few kings in my day
And I wish them all straight to hell

Because Kings don't need queens
They needs servants on knees
Bowed down and bent low
For Kings' glory to show

I have known many kings
Seen their glory proclaimed
And their need for subservience
Crowned me in shame

It was kings on their thrones
With no rules but their own
That used me as a child
And Kings on their thrones
With no rules but their own
That chose me to defile

And while the crowds sang their praise
I prayed each night to find my grave
Cuz servants have no rights, you see
No court of peers to hear their plea
No voice to beg for clemency
No shouts for mercy to be free
Can be heard above the drone
Of chants to kings upon their throne

Years ago I married a king
And quickly learned that my new ring
Really only meant one thing
I was now the King's new bitch
To be used to scratch his royal itch
To fuck or suck upon command

And when I tried to find my feet
He doubled down on my defeat
The words from his lips
His kingdom defined
And whipped and lashed and bent my spine

I left his kingdom
In bright daylight
The child in my belly
Gave me strength to fight
For to mother a prince
Had at last made me queen

But he was not the last king I would meet
Just walk out this door and look down the street
The light reflected from a thousand crowns
Outshines sun and moon
And in oceans of testosterone drowns
My hope

My hope of one day finding a man
Who wants me on my feet
To stand with him, beside him
Not bowed cheek to feet

I have one King who reigns supreme
My knees bend to Him alone
My God and my King who made me a queen
Not to bow at some lowly man's throne

But he made me a woman
With a woman's needs
And a heart full of love
To give and receive

He made me a poet
With a passion for truth
Not passion for boy kings
Still locked in their youth

But living in this land of kings
I will always be left alone
For no self-appointed king
Will I bow to a motherfuckin' throne

My Muse

Stopped at the drug store
On my way home tonight
Bought an ounce of pride
And a lick of sense
Damn that shit's expensive

Saw a ten pound bag of shame
In the next aisle
But I left that there
I keep a storeroom full of that shit at home

Wish I'd thought to return
The other things I bought
After the famous date
What the fuck am I going to do
With an unopened box
Of Tropical flavored condoms
(I told him we'd match)
And the large size box of Prevacid
I don't have fucking reflux

They're in a bag in my closet
Along with the freshly laundered
And now officially retired
Blue lace thong

Out of sight out of mind
That was the plan
Too bad that doesn't actually work
When the mind is mine
Anyway…I wonder if I can find the receipt?

I think we'll call it a fair trade
I mean
The sex was exceptional
I may be out of practice
But that shit was outstanding
Just the memory makes me wet

Not to mention the going rate
For a muse these days
Ten days of girlish glee
One incredible night
Three weeks of sobbing
Adds up to twelve poems
Twelve fucking poems
They should have charged more
For the ounce of pride

He was a cyber promise
He was unexpected blessings
Left me sleepless
He was light in my dark night
Left me praying
In a sea of tears
Enticing hope
He was flame
Caused rivers to flow
Tempted dark dances
To the memory of his smile

Cadence

And I was
A wet and willing woman
With too much baggage to bear
Too much crazy for care
And storerooms of shame
To my name

Be careful what you wish for
I wished for a mechanic
And I got one
Only I mistook him for more.

One In Four

Please give a hand to all the ladies in the house
Look at how we come in every form and fashion
From the earth mother and the shy, bookish mouse
To the hot sexy mama that boldly incites your passion

Take a good close look at these ladies and tell me who you see
Does she remind you of your Mama, little sister or your Auntie?
Do you look into her eyes or just between her thighs
Where you want your dick to be?

Can any of you tell
Which face is masking hell
Statistics say that one in four ladies that you see
Lives her life trapped in hell, longing to be free

Are you looking more closely now?
Is that a bruise beneath her eye?
How did she really get that scar?
Trust me it is the scars that you will never see
That makes us who we are

It is the faceless man with enormous hands
That touched her when she was four
That son of Satan in command
Behind her marriage door

Broken bones may be set and made whole
Bruises may fade and beauty restore
Not so for the beaten ravaged souls
Of the one in four

Cadence

Are you looking more closely now?
Could she be the pretty clerk at the liquor store
Could she be the one in four?
Was she your last quick fuck on a darkened street?
Or perhaps the very next enchanting lady that you meet

When she was kneeling at your feet
And blowing you so sweet, so sweet
Did she hear his voice inside her head
Suck me bitch or you'll wish you were dead

Can you ever know how he fucked with her head?
How many night she lay in bed
Choking on the shame that she'd been fed
Praying to God that she'd wake up dead

Are you looking more closely now?
Do you see her in me?

Will you be both her lover and her friend
Will you stand for her and her honor defend
Will you give her the love that she needs to mend
Will you banish her shame and help suffering to end

Take a good close look at these ladies, and tell me who you see
Does she remind you of your Mama, little sister or your Auntie?
Will you look into her eyes or just between her thighs
Where you want your dick to be?

Financial Reform

Forty-three years ago
God, in His wisdom
Opened a new off-shore bank account
And he called the account Giselle

Over the years this account has seen a whole lot of activity
There have been many deposits
Nourishment and education
Love and support
That being said
One might expect that this account
Would have shown steady and consistent growth over the years
And that might have been true
Had it not been for the endless withdrawals
And periodic fraudulent charges posted to the Giselle account

Normal expenditures of love and support
Nourishment and education
Care and affection
Should have been covered
Under God's beginning balance of grace
And the expected deposits

But this world is filled
With thieves and shysters
Players and parlay-ers
Always ready and willing
To steal your treasure
For their own selfish pleasure
And they have hit the Giselle account
Time and time again

They stole joy
They stole pleasure
Stole peace in endless measure
Posted fraudulent charges
To accounts called Abuse and Neglect
And plain old Hate
Caused overdrafts of
Pain and Tears and Grief

But due to the recent financial crisis
My president has passed new banking reforms
And established the Consumer Protection Agency
To put an end to this abuse

So here are the new rules for the Giselle account
If you don't make a deposit
You can't make a withdrawal
Let me say that again
If you don't put none in
You cyan take none out
Your credentials will be checked and re-checked by the teller
The ATM is closed
This is not an Easy Access account
Only Certified Depositors will be granted access
But interest will be compounded in Truth and in Grace

So, if you've come to steal my joy
And brought me only strife
Keep your thievin' hands off my account
And stay the hell out of my life

Declaration Of Independence

On this day I swear
I do hereby declare
My independence from fear
I free my pen and my tongue
From the only topic I had called taboo
And it was only ever taboo
Because I was so scared of you

Scared that these words
Would color your view
Of what I say, what I do
Who you see from this day
But if these words
Affect your respect for me
I don't really want it anyway
Emergency exits are at the back
So see if you can find your way

I am Bipolar
Sorry
I have Bipolar Disorder
As the poets will tell you
It matters how you say it
To be clear I don't have it a little bit
I live with mountains of this shit
Uncle Sam don't send me a check every month
Because I'm his favorite

By now some of you have done the math
And already found me lacking
So I'll address the rest
To those of you who are still
Reserving judgment

Cadence

Who the hell do you think you are
To judge me anyway
I wake up each and everyday
To see what this curse will bring
The color of the hell I will visit today
Will it be bright red and so manic
That I want to jump out of my skin
Or the blue-black dark of midday night
When not to end my life I fight
Or the need to lock myself in
And throw away the key
Or just maybe it will be
The calm the peaceful green
Of that middle I forever desire
More than likely it will be
The rollercoaster ride
That I'll exhaust myself trying to hide
From you

I once had a doctor who said
He'd like to put casts on his patients' heads
Because when people can see
That someone is hurt that something is broken
They understand, respect, lend a helping hand

Never broke a bone
But labeled disabled
This curse is incurable
And no fault of my own
Yet, still it's viewed as shameful
As though to you I should atone

You, who sit and judge
You, who will now question
My joy or my tears
You, who will never know
That my 44 years
Are a miracle of survival
You, who will hear mental
Not illness

Ignorance of the facts
Is no excuse for your crime
But there it is nevertheless
Some folks will never learn
What they do not want to know
What can I say
There is no cure for stupid
To quote the poet GF Soldier
"If you can't say Amen
Just say ouch"

My only child has the very same illness
The doctors think it will kill him
Cancer or Bipolar
From illness of the blood
Or illness of the brain
Dead is dead

So it is from you
Whom I now declare
My blessed independence
To all the others - Thank you
Judge me now
Judge me now

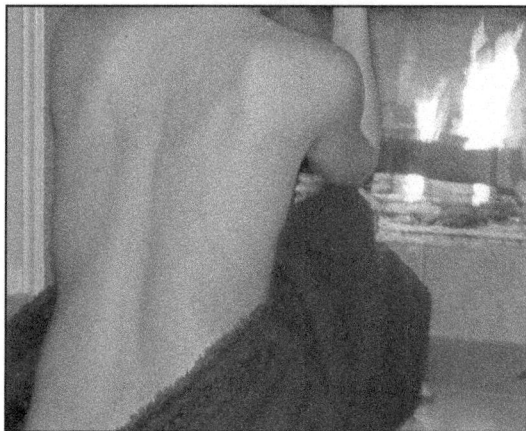

~ *five* ~
Poet's Fuel
(A Bit of Suffering is Mandatory)

Haiku

My scars are wider

Than the wounds that they came from

'Cause I pick my scabs

~

Haiku

We all have baggage

Mine holds shattered pieces that

Once were confidence

Mirror

She was made
A mirror
Allowed only
To possess
What was
Reflected
On her
In her.

Parents
Looked down
So tired
They frowned
No baby
Not now
No time
No patience
For another child
They laid
The tracks
For cracks
To come.

Big sisters
Saw baby
A live toy
Just maybe
But mostly
A bother
A fly
In adolescent
Cream pie

Leaving trails
Where she
Would break
One day.

The men
They came
They looked
With lust
Then touched
Her youth
And hushed
She cracked.

She grew
And cried
She told
They said
She lied
So she lay
In bed
And tried
To die.

She woke
They said
Her glass
Was broke
And so
She lived
Broken
Still trying
Still hoping
For a token
Of affection.

Now grown
They came
One by one
And her
Cracked glass
Absorbed
Their sun
She shimmered
And shone
And tried
To atone
For the fact
That she
Was broken
But the
Irregularities
In her
Reflection
Did not
Merit
Their affection
And so
They left
They left
New cracks.

He was
Born past
Midnight
Her baby.
At dawn
She woke
He's sick
They said
So sick.

She feared
He bore
The reflection
Of her sin
She prayed
She cried
They stitched
They sewed
They mended
He'd grow
Just fine
They said
But they
Could not
Yet know
His mind
His mind
Beheld
All the cracks
That in
Her dwelled
Only magnified.

As one
By one
Those cracks
Revealed
And doctors
Said
They could
Not heal
So she
Loved
She loved
Those cracks

Like hers
That had
Always
Kept love
From her
Her days
Penance
Her nights
Hell.

She wrote
She spoke
Was bathed
In new light
This hue
Neither red
Nor blue
But warm
And welcome.

Warmth
So foreign
So long
Unknown
For cracks
She'd held
Like shame
Those scars
Symbols
Of imperfections
Founded in
Reflections
Of all those
That had come
Before
Now drew
Hugs from
Strangers

Hugs
Held power
To mend glass
Like injections
Of resin
Into her
Broken places
'Til at times
She began
To feel
More whole.

But she
Was made
A mirror
Knows no
Other way
Of seeing
Reflecting
Is being
So she still
Cracks
At frowns
At drawn brows
At rejection.

She
Was made
A mirror.

Shackles

There've been times
When I've struggled and fought
Clamored and clawed
To dig my way out of this dark hole
Bloodied hands
Drenched in sweat
Times when I've immersed in prayer
Bathed in the promise of hope
Sought the good
As though positive thoughts
Words, deeds
Would levitate my soul
From the depths of this dark hole
But shiny hope
Nor bloody hands
Can free me
From these shackles
That keep me trapped
In this dark place
Never quite letting the light
Reach my face
So - Remove the shackles
So simple you say
Free yourself
Move on
Live life
Praise God
Be grateful
For this day

And when I explain
Call my shackles by name
My only son
My sweet baby boy
Who's known so much
More pain than joy
Seems to bear the Curse
Damned to only get – Worse
No
There can be no warm sunlight
Only the icy dark of endless night
Shackles
Not my feet
But on my soul
Condemn me
To remain
Forever
Crying
Dying
In the dark

So They Say

They say
What don't kill you makes you stronger
How fucking strong do I need to be?

They say God hears a Mother's tears
Hello! – You're not listening

They say the definition of insanity is
Doing the same thing over and over
And expecting a different result

So I dream a different dream
Say a different prayer
Wish a smaller wish
And hope
Hope for any little success

But still
Crying
Knowing
God's not hearing

I wish
And dream
And pray
And hope
And try
God knows I try

And if that don't meet your fucking definition of crazy
I don't know what does

Mercy

Poems to empty rooms
Ode to a dark and hollow soul
Rhythms only in my mind
Use the poets' silent rhyme
To pen on pages
The tortures of time

Time, the greatest teacher
Wounder, Healer
No. That's right
There is no healing here
No hope for healing
But prayer
Not prayer for healing
But prayer that time
Would cease
To be
That to me
Was Mercy

Haunted

I am haunted
By a trio of ghosts
They have been with me
For as long as I can remember
Caused pain beyond measure
They cannot be exorcised
By priest or potion
They are unmoved by callused knees
And tired raspy voice
By countless prayers and pleas
In dark night and desperate days
I have run from my tormentors
Packed lock, stock and barrel
Moved to the frozen north
Fled to the arid south
They hide in the folds of my clothes
In the lids of my eyes
So no matter how far I run
They find me
Have you seen them?
The one called No one
Has stolen the love of my lovers
For decades
She says having No one is always preferable
To having me
Her sister Nothing is the answer
To what my efforts were lacking
Says nothing I do will make me worthy

Sister number three, Love
Spills from my pores
Falls unwanted
Puddles at my feet
Reflecting failure
In the light of sun and moon
My ghostly trio
Are stone cold
And unrelenting
I despise them
With everything in me
And still I have nowhere to hide

Hightide

The moon held sway
Washing craggy shores
In waves of ocean foam.
Their meeting was
As ever
Overwhelming
Neither sea nor shore
Could deny the lunar call.
As time and tide
Recede
Leaving behind
Wet sand and sheets
Sea and shore
Return with a sigh
To their comfort zone
Both taking and leaving
Pieces of the other.
More at ease
But strangely missing
The tumult
Of their joining.
Powerless as they were
To resist her call
They can now only wait
For her return.
There is an immeasurable expanse
Of sea blue sheet between them
Drier now
With the passing of the night.

So they wait
Certain that she will return
At the call of the moon
Wishing she could know
That he would welcome
Her return
Or come to her
By sheer will of his own.

At Sea

When my well is empty
But for my tears
When it is capped off
For tears remain
Unwanted
Unneeded
Unheeded

I can only
Bathe in them
As they multiply
One times one
Welcomes none

Until I am forced to swim
As the level rises
Past my heart
Drip no more
For cheeks soaked

Tears still flow
In oceans
Of salt

I know not
What makes me
Swim
Toward air

Knowing more
Pain and tears
Wait there

Unwanted
Unneeded
Unheeded

I breathe
I cry
I want
I need
I thirst
I crave
I pray
And wait
And swim
And swim

Sweet Amnesia

Sometimes
Once in awhile
When I am safe
When I am alone
In my four walls
I forget
To remember

Sometimes
When I close my eyes
And allow sweet sleep
To claim me
I forget
To remember

Sometimes
In silence
In the dark
In the flow of my pen
I forget
To remember

And in those moments
Of sweet forgetting
I am beautiful
I am strong
I am healthy
I am worthy
I can do all things
Be all things

My mirror sings praises
Pages shout accolades
Blood sings in my veins
God is Love

Sometimes
Once in awhile
When I am safe
When I am alone
In my four walls
In sleep
In dreams
In silence
In the dark
In the flow of my pen
I forget
To remember

Where Truth Lies

When you touch me
Is it truly the most magnificent burn?
Or have I just been
So cold for so long
That the warmth of your fingertips
Feels like I am engulfed in flame?

When you love me
Give me words
Give me you
Is this heartbeat
That reverberates
Through all of me
True?
Or the gratitude
Of a yearning heart
So starved for love
It beat not red but blue?

When they support the heart of me
The art of me
When in them I see
A match. A fit.
A home for me
Tho the accolades and praise
Sound like clanging clashing cymbals
Chafing to eardrums that have only known
Criticism and censure
Is it home I have found
Or just a temporary illusion
Of hard surface
Over the boggy ground that birthed me
Nursed me
Cursed me?

Is the wonder of my new world
So wonderful at all?
Or is it just the years of wandering
That let all my hopes fall?
And so to my parched and dying soul
This is manna
Rainfalls of Blessings
Sent on wings
From God above.

Am I so truly Blessed
Or just thought so little of myself
That I am now drowning in an excess
Of thankfulness?

Nectar Memories

Your well once fed
Like the freshest of springs
Like the nectar of gods
After eons of muddy offerings.
But it has been rancid
For some time now.
Still I return
Time and again
Lured by remnant memory
Lingering taste of nectar
Shocked each time
As vinegar washes over tongue
Throat clenching
Against it's acrid, bitter taste
Each time I promise to remember
This well is poison to me
Each time I return
Spirit still yearns
For elusive sweetness found
In nectar memories

A Prayer Of Gratitude

The road from
Then to now
Was long
And unthinkably hard

There was no light at the end of the tunnel
The clouds lining was as ominous as the rest
The glass was neither half full nor half empty
But irreparably cracked and seeping life's blood

Death stared me down
His. Then mine
Day and night
Night and day
Time had no meaning anyway

'I am talking about your son in a grave'
He'd say
'So how can you stand to hear me speak?'
I said I had no choice
If I fell, who would stand for him?

Only for God
Would I fall to my knees
And plead for my son's life
'Oh sweet Jesus, please'

But I prayed without hope
As I worked without end
Though I had all faith in God
Years of prayers as he got worse
Said to me this was my curse
My cross to bear

Cadence

Priests could only speak of Job
Of martyrs and of saints
The mere mention of Abraham
Left me feeling faint

I am not Abraham I cried
Though abandoned from every side
Not Job nor a saint
As I pled for the life of my child

His voice came through my door tonight
A movie captured his delight
As I lay with the man I love
A raucous laugh
A goofy giggle
Disturbed the peaceful night

Safe and sound
Whole and well
And just as crazy
As an 18 yr old should be

No one looks at us
And sees the scars
Of our journey through hell

But I know
Yes Lord, I know
That when I lost my hope
You held it safe for me
Amen

The Dance

I no longer recall
The first notes of the song
The first steps of the dance
The first glimpse of my lover's face

It matters not
How it began
From whence he came
At this stage of our embrace

Though many years have passed
He still comes to me in darkness
Always watching me from shadows
Ever willing and ready to resume the dance

Our steps fall as one
Synchronized by time
Choreography beautifully honed
Over countless dark nights

Familiar notes
Haunting harmonies
His darkness to mine
Embrace, invite, entice

Swirling now
Countenance blurs
Drums beat
Toward crescendo

And I awake
From his spell
Mists flung aside
As tho' by the hand of God

Cadence

As dawn comes
As dawn always does
Death's dark beauty fades

Notes linger still
A vaguely remembered melody
Muscles ache from the exertion of the dance
The swirl of thoughts is slower to still
Than skirts

As the sun rises in the sky
It is harder to remember why
My lover came this time

It pains me not to see him go
Another dance survived
But lessons learned through time and trial
We'll dance again in darkest night

Hawk And Hummingbird

I would love to soar like hawk
But hummingbird be me
Perpetual motion enchants human eye
Tired spirit eyes cannot see

As I poise before this flower
A thousand beats per hour
Be the price of its nectar
My world. My wings.
Be beating. Unceasing.

I sense the hawk above
Massive wings catch winds and soar
Soar with elegant, effortless grace
Queen of skies suspends time in space

No meager flower fuels her power
Servant skies give rise to wings
Give shine to predator's eyes

I dream that I might soar like hawk
But hummingbird be me

About The Author

Giselle Robinson... Rock City Poet

Giselle Robinson was born in "Rock City", St. Thomas, USVI. Giselle's voice and her words, her stories and her style, reflect the deeply ingrained West Indian values and traditions she was raised with. She is as warm and smooth, deep and as vibrant as the Caribbean Sea.

She and her son have lived in Fort Worth for 4 yrs. This is where she was first introduced to the open mic in September 2009.

DFW's own Island Girl, Giselle is a member of the 2011 and 2012 Fort Worth Slam Teams as well as the 2011 DFW Gladiator Slam Champion. Representing Dallas, she ranked 31st in World at the 2012 Women of the World Poetry Slam Championship. She has also released her first CD and DVD of poems from "Cadence".

Giselle says she writes because she has to, is compelled to, but she performs for that moment of personal connection; shared pain, shared purpose. She's still amused by reactions to her accent; after all, it's just "Me".